EAU CLAIRE DISTRICT LIBRARY
6528 East Main Street
P.O. Box 328
EAU CLAIRE, MI 49111

J
513.2
Mid

W9-BAI-184

JOSEPH MIDTHUN   SAMUEL HITI

BUILDING BLOCKS OF MATHEMATICS

SUBTRACTION

WORLD
BOOK

a Scott Fetzer company
Chicago

www.worldbook.com

EAU CLAIRE DISTRICT LIBRARY

World Book 12-16-13 $25.00

World Book, Inc.
233 N. Michigan Avenue
Chicago, IL 60601
U.S.A.

For information about other World Book publications,
visit our website at www.worldbook.com
or call 1-800-WORLDBK (967-5325).
For information about sales to schools and libraries,
call 1-800-975-3250 (United States),
or 1-800-837-5365 (Canada).

©2013 World Book, Inc. All rights reserved. This volume
may not be reproduced in whole or in part in any form
without prior written permission from the publisher.

WORLD BOOK and the GLOBE DEVICE are registered
trademarks or trademarks of World Book, Inc.

Library of Congress Cataloging-in-Publication Data

Subtraction.
     pages cm -- (Building blocks of mathematics)
     Summary: "A graphic nonfiction volume that
introduces critical basic subtraction concepts"--
Provided by publisher.
     Includes index.
     ISBN 978-0-7166-1437-1 -- ISBN 978-0-7166-1478-4 (pbk.)
     1. Subtraction--Comic books, strips, etc.--
Juvenile literature. 2. Graphic novels. I. World
Book, Inc.
     QA115.S856 2013
     513.2'12--dc23
                              2012031040

Building Blocks of Mathematics
ISBN: 978-0-7166-1431-9 (set, hc.)

Printed in China by Shenzhen Donnelley
Printing Co., Ltd., Guangdong Province
2nd printing October 2013

Acknowledgments:
Created by Samuel Hiti and Joseph Midthun
Art by Samuel Hiti
Written by Joseph Midthun
Special thanks to Anita Wager, Hala
Ghousseini, and Syril McNally.

STAFF

Executive Committee
President: Donald D. Keller
Vice President and Editor in Chief:
   Paul A. Kobasa
Vice President, Sales & Marketing:
   Sean Lockwood
Vice President, International: Richard Flower
Director, Human Resources: Bev Ecker

Editorial
Manager, Series and Trade: Cassie Mayer
Writer and Letterer: Joseph Midthun
Manager, Contracts & Compliance
   (Rights & Permissions): Loranne K. Shields

Manufacturing/Pre-Press
Director: Carma Fazio
Manufacturing Manager: Steven Hueppchen
Production/Technology Manager:
   Anne Fritzinger
Proofreader: Emilie Schrage

Graphics and Design
Senior Manager, Graphics and Design: Tom Evan
Coordinator, Design Development and
   Production: Brenda B. Tropinski
Book Design: Samuel Hiti

TABLE OF CONTENTS

CHECKING YOUR WORK

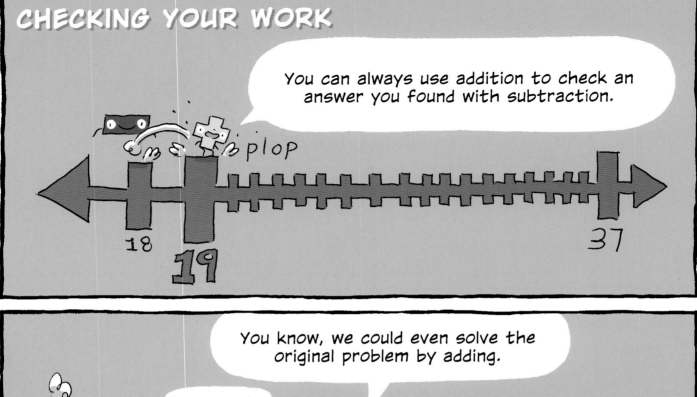

You can always use addition to check an answer you found with subtraction.

You know, we could even solve the original problem by adding.

No way!

Sure.

I'd write the problem like this:

Now we just need to count up from 19 until we reach 37.

Lead the way.

I need some more bait!

WHIP

ZZZ

PlOP

How many worms do we have left?

Hold on—I'll count.

Hmm. *15!*

Whoops!

Oh no!

TUNK

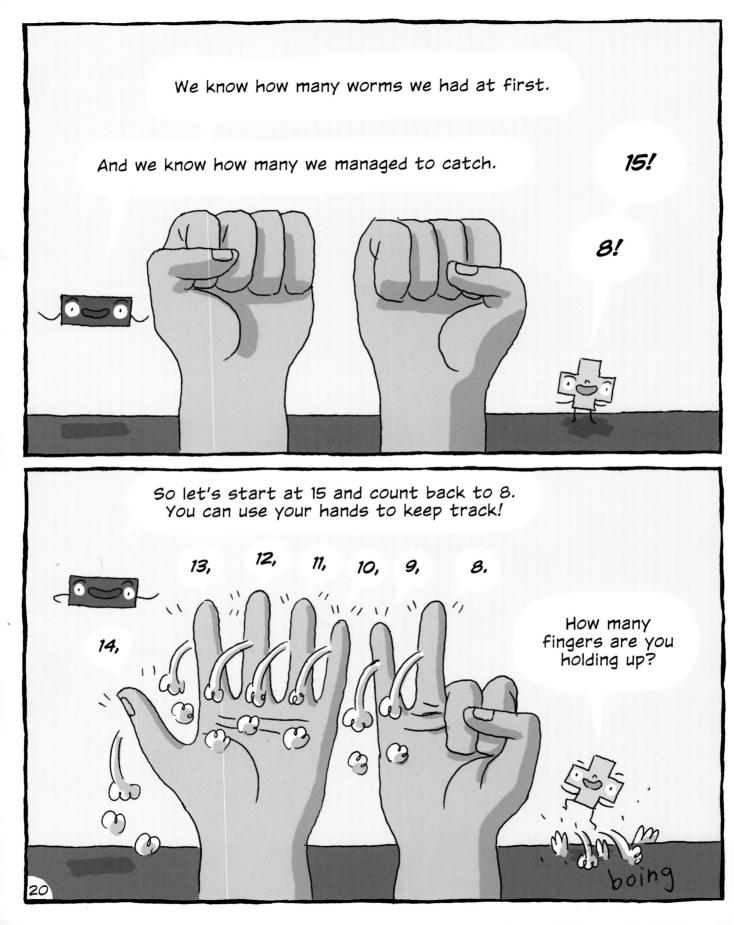

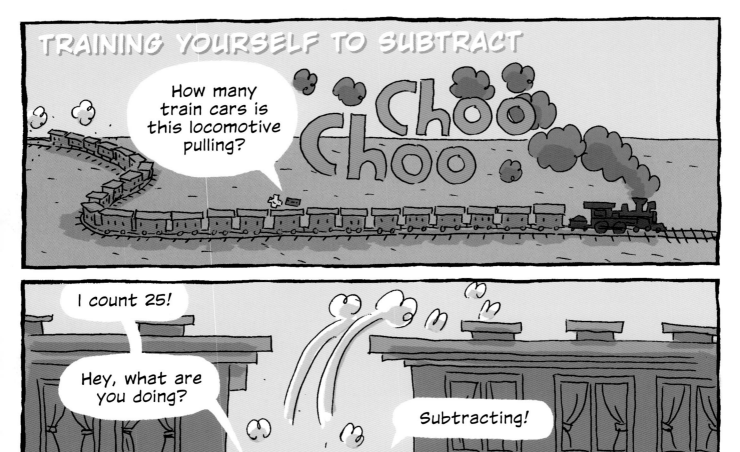

How many train cars is this locomotive pulling?

Choo Choo Choo

I count 25!

Hey, what are you doing?

Subtracting!

ping

What?

How many cars did you subtract?

SUBTRACTION FACTS

This table below can help you add and subtract fast!
It can also help you learn your subtraction fact families.
A fact family shows how groups of numbers are related.

The table shows 10 different fact families for addition and subtraction. Can you think of more fact families?

5 + 5 = 10 10 - 5 = 5	6 + 5 = 11 11 - 5 = 6 11 - 6 = 5	7 + 5 = 11 12 - 5 = 7 12 - 7 = 5	8 + 5 = 13 13 - 5 = 8 13 - 8 = 5	9 + 5 = 14 14 - 5 = 9 14 - 9 = 5
5 + 6 = 11 11 - 6 = 5 11 - 5 = 6	6 + 6 = 12 12 - 6 = 6	7 + 6 = 13 13 - 6 = 7 13 - 7 = 6	8 + 6 = 14 14 - 6 = 8 14 - 8 = 6	9 + 6 = 15 15 - 6 = 9 15 - 9 = 6
5 + 7 = 12 12 - 7 = 5 12 - 5 = 7	6 + 7 = 13 13 - 7 = 6 13 - 6 = 7	7 + 7 = 14 14 - 7 = 7	8 + 7 = 15 15 - 7 = 8 15 - 8 = 7	9 + 7 = 16 16 - 7 = 9 16 - 9 = 7
5 + 8 = 13 13 - 8 = 5 13 - 5 = 8	6 + 8 = 14 14 - 8 = 6 14 - 6 = 8	7 + 8 = 15 15 - 8 = 7 15 - 7 = 8	8 + 8 = 16 16 - 8 = 8	9 + 8 = 17 17 - 8 = 9 17 - 9 = 8
5 + 9 = 14 14 - 9 = 5 14 - 5 = 9	6 + 9 = 15 15 - 9 = 6 15 - 6 = 9	7 + 9 = 16 16 - 9 = 7 16 - 7 = 9	8 + 9 = 17 17 - 9 = 8 17 - 8 = 9	9 + 9 = 18 18 - 9 = 9

FIND OUT MORE

BOOKS

The Action of Subtraction
by Brian Cleary and Brian Gable
(Millbrook Press, 2006)

Help Me Learn Subtraction
by Jean Marzollo
and Chad Phillips
(Holiday House, 2012)

If You Were a Minus Sign
by Trisha Speed Shaskan
and Francesca Carabelli
(Picture Window Books, 2009)

**Panda Math: Learning About
Subtraction from Hua Mei
and Mei Sheng**
by Ann Whitehead Nagda
(Henry Holt, 2005)

Pet Store Subtraction
by Simone T. Ribke
(Children's Press, 2007)

**Subtracting with Sebastian Pig
and Friends: On a Camping Trip**
by Jill Anderson
and Amy Huntington
(Enslow Publishers, 2009)

Subtraction at School
by Jennifer Rozines Roy
and Gregory Roy (Marshall
Cavendish Benchmark, 2006)

Subtraction Made Easy
by Rebecca Wingard-Nelson
and Tom LaBaff
(Enslow Elementary, 2005)

**What's the Difference? An Endangered
Animal Subtraction Story**
by Suzanne Slade and Joan C. Waites
(Sylvan Dell Publishing, 2010)

WEBSITES

Cool Math 4 Kids: Subtraction
www.coolmath4kids.com/subtraction/
Lessons, practice activities, and flash
cards help kids improve their
subtraction skills.

Fun 4 the Brain: Subtraction
www.fun4thebrain.com/subtraction.html
This educational website includes games
and printable worksheets that teach
the basics of subtraction strategies.

Gamequarium
www.gamequarium.com/subtraction.html
This teacher-designed website
provides many pages of games for
practice with subtraction, addition,
and other math skills.

Kids' Numbers
www.kidsnumbers.com/subtraction.php
Prepare with week-by-week subtraction
lessons, and practice your skills with
a wide variety of subtraction games.

Math Blaster
www.mathblaster.com/
parents/math-games
Math games for all skill sets and
all primary grades can be found
at this website.

Math Nook: Subtraction Games
www.mathnook.com/math/skill/
subtractiongames.php
Fun and challenging games for all ages
teach and sharpen subtraction skills.

NOTE TO EDUCATORS

This volume supports a conceptual understanding of subtraction through a series of story problems. As the Subtraction character solves each story problem, it presents different strategies, including variations of direct modeling, counting, and invented strategies. Below is an index of strategies that appear in this volume. For more information about how to use these strategies in the classroom, see the list of Educator Resources at the bottom of this page.

Index of Strategies

Educator Resources

Children's Mathematics: Cognitively Guided Instruction
    by Thomas Carpenter, Elizabeth Fennema, Megan L. Franke, Linda Levi, and Susan B. Empson (Heinemann, 1999)

Elementary and Middle School Mathematics: Teaching Developmentally
    by John A. Van de Walle, Karen S. Karp, and Jennifer M. Bay-Williams (Harcourt, 2013)

Knowing and Teaching Elementary Mathematics: Teachers' Understanding of Fundamental Mathematics in China and the United States
    by Liping Ma (Routledge, 2010)

Young Mathematicians at Work:
Constructing Number Sense, Addition, and Subtraction
    by Catherine Twomey Fosnot and Maarten Dolk (Heinemann, 2011)

EAU CLAIRE DISTRICT LIBRARY